NEVER SWIM ALONE &
THIS IS A PLAY

Never Swim Alone &
This Is A Play

Daniel MacIvor

Playwrights Canada Press
Toronto

For professional or amateur production rights, please contact:
The Gary Goddard Agency
149 Church Street, 2nd Floor
Toronto, ON M5B 1Y4
416-928-0299, meaghan@garygoddardagency.com

LIBRARY AND ARCHIVES CANADA CATALOGUING IN PUBLICATION
MacIvor, Daniel, 1962-
[Plays. Selections]
    Never swim alone ; &, This is a play / Daniel MacIvor. -- Second edition.

Plays.
Contents: Never swim alone -- This is a play.
Issued in print and electronic formats.
ISBN 978-1-77091-462-9 (paperback).--ISBN 978-1-77091-463-6 (pdf).--
ISBN 978-1-77091-464-3 (epub).--ISBN 978-1-77091-465-0 (mobi)

    I. MacIvor, Daniel, 1962- . Never swim alone. II. MacIvor, Daniel, 1962- .
This is a play. III. Title.

PS8575.I86A6 2015   C812'.54   C2015-904064-7
                                                     C2015-904065-5

We acknowledge the financial support of the Canada Council for the Arts, the Ontario Arts Council (OAC), the Ontario Media Development Corporation, and the Government of Canada through the Canada Book Fund for our publishing activities. Nous remercions l'appui financier du Conseil des Arts du Canada, le Conseil des Arts de l'Ontario (CAO), la Société de développement de l'industrie des médias de l'Ontario, et le Gouvernement du Canada par l'entremise du Fonds du livre du Canada pour nos activités d'édition.

 Canada Council   Conseil des arts
for the Arts   du Canada

 ONTARIO ARTS COUNCIL
CONSEIL DES ARTS DE L'ONTARIO
an Ontario government agency
un organisme du gouvernement de l'Ontario

 Canada

 Ontario
Ontario Media Development
Corporation

Never Swim Alone

with love to Ken McDougall,
a formidable foe and friend indeed

Never Swim Alone was written in residence at Tarragon Theatre and subsequently workshopped at VideoCabaret with Earl Pastko, Daniel Brooks and G.B. Jones. The play was first produced by Platform 9 Theatre in association with da da kamera at the Theatre Centre, Queen Street West, Toronto. It opened on February 26, 1991, with the following cast and creative team:

Referee: Caroline Gillis
A. Francis Delorenzo: Robert Dodds
William (Bill) Wade: Daniel MacIvor

Directed by Ken McDougall
Designed by Steve Lucas
Stage managed by Anne Driscoll

Characters

Referee: A girl in a blue bathing suit.
A. Francis Delorenzo: A man in a suit.
William (Bill) Wade: An almost imperceptibly
shorter man in a suit.

Up stage centre sits a tall chair (maybe a lifeguard chair, maybe a director's chair); stage left sits a chair for BILL, a briefcase beside it; stage right is a chair for FRANK, a briefcase beside it. As the audience enters the girl lies on stage under a sheet (perhaps she is mostly unnoticed by the audience). Nostalgic summer music plays.

FRANK and BILL enter through the house, greeting the audience and singling people out: "Hey, glad you could come." "Nice to see you again." "That's a great shirt." "Call me Friday," etc. They step on stage and turn to the audience.

FRANK **&** BILL
(in unison) Hello.
Good to see you.
Glad you could come.

They slowly lift the sheet from the REFEREE. She rises. She wears a blue bathing suit. She looks out and steps down centre.

REFEREE

A beach.

A bay.

The point.

Two boys on a beach. Late afternoon. They have been here all day, and they have been here all day every day all summer. It is the last day of summer before school begins. Nearby is a girl. She as well has been here all day, and all day every day all summer. She lies on her green beach towel in her blue bathing suit with her yellow radio. The boys have been watching the girl from a distance all summer, but now that the summer is nearly over, the boys are braver and watch from very close by. She reminds one boy of his sister; she reminds the other of a picture of a woman he once saw in a magazine. She thinks the boys are funny. She thinks the boys are cute. She turns her head a little over her shoulder and speaks to the boys: "Race you to the point?"

This is the beach.

Here is the bay.

There is the point.

> *FRANK and BILL sit. The REFEREE steps to her chair and puts on a whistle. She sits. She blows her whistle.*

Round One: Stature.

The REFEREE blows her whistle to begin Round One.

FRANK and BILL rise and step forward.

FRANK & BILL

Two men enter a room.

FRANK

Good to see you, Bill.

BILL

Good to see you, Frank.

FRANK

How long's it been?

BILL

Weeks?

FRANK

Months?

BILL

Too long, Frank.

FRANK

Too long indeed, Bill.

FRANK & BILL

How's things? Can't complain. How's the family? Just great. How's business? Well a whole heck of a lot better then it was this time last year let me tell you. Ha ha ha.

How's the blood pressure?

(aside and snide) Ha ha ha.

FRANK

Two men.

BILL

Two men.

FRANK & BILL

Two men enter a room. A taller man and—

> *They stop. They laugh. As they speak they each gesture that he is the taller man.*

A taller man and—

A taller man and—'

A taller man and—

A taller man and—

> *The REFEREE blows her whistle to end the round. The men stand side by side facing her. She steps down and inspects them carefully, measuring their height. She stands between the two men, holding their arms. After a moment she lifts FRANK's arm, giving him the victory. BILL takes his seat. FRANK steps front and centre and addresses the audience.*

FRANK

A. Francis Delorenzo. My friends call me Frank. The "A" is for Alphonse and not even my enemies call me Alphonse. Alphonse Francis Delorenzo: French, English, Italian. Behold before you a square of the Canadian quilt. To those of you I didn't have a chance to greet as I entered I'd like to say welcome and thank you for coming. I'm sure you all have busy schedules and many other concerns in these troubled times and your presence here tonight is greatly appreciated. A hand for the audience! And if I might I would like to start off with a favourite quote of mine: "We do not place especial value on the possession of virtue until we notice its total absence in our opponent." Friedrich Nietzsche. Once again, thanks for coming.

> *FRANK resumes his seat.*

REFEREE

Round Two: Uniform.

The REFEREE blows her whistle to begin Round Two.

FRANK & BILL

Two men enter a room.

FRANK

A taller man and

BILL

an almost imperceptibly shorter man.

FRANK

They both wear

FRANK & BILL

White shirts. Blue suits. Silk ties. Black shoes. Black socks.
White shirts, blue suits, silk ties, black shoes, black socks.
Whiteshirts bluesuits silkties blackshoes blacksocks.
Whiteshirtsbluesuitssilktiesblackshoesblacksockswhiteshirtsblue
suitssilktiesblackshoesblacksocks. White shirts:

BILL

A hundred and ten twenty-five at Harry Rosen's.

FRANK & BILL

Blue suits:

FRANK

Nine twenty-two twenty-two

BILL

on sale

FRANK

at Dugger's.

FRANK & BILL

Silk ties:

BILL

came with the suit?

FRANK

Present.

BILL

From Donna?

FRANK

Ah . . . no.

BILL

Oh. It's nice.

FRANK

How's Sally?

BILL

Oh good good. How's Donna?

FRANK

Oh good good.

BILL

How's the house?

FRANK

Very good.

FRANK & BILL

How's the boy? Just fine. Now there's an investment, huh?

FRANK

Three?

BILL

Four. Five?

FRANK

Four.

FRANK & BILL

Right right. Good kid? Great kid. Smart kid? A little genius. Must get it from his mother. Ha ha ha ha ha ha ha. Black shoes:

FRANK

Two twenty-five even, David's uptown.

FRANK & BILL

Black socks:

BILL

(excitedly noting FRANK's socks) BLUE SOCKS!

The REFEREE blows her whistle. She steps down and inspects the men's socks. She gives the victory to BILL. FRANK takes his seat. BILL steps out and addresses the audience.

Hello to all the familiar faces in the audience tonight and a very extra hello to all the friends I haven't met yet. William (Bill) Wade: Canadian, Canadian, Canadian. That's what's beautiful about this country: doesn't matter where you come from, once you're here you're a Canadian, and that makes me proud. And I'd also like to add a bit of a quote myself, as my old man always used to say: "If bullshit had a brain it would quote Nietzsche." Thank you.

REFEREE
Round Three: Who Falls Dead The Best.

The REFEREE blows her whistle to begin the round.

FRANK and BILL step forward with their briefcases.

FRANK & BILL
Two men enter a room.

BILL
And each man carries

FRANK & BILL

a briefcase.

FRANK

The first man seems very much like the second man and

BILL

the first man seems very much like the second man.

FRANK & BILL

Yes.

FRANK

But

BILL

they

FRANK

are

FRANK & BILL

not.

FRANK

For two reasons.

BILL

Two.

FRANK

One:

FRANK & BILL

one man is the first man and

BILL

two:

FRANK & BILL

one man in his briefcase has

FRANK

a gun.

BILL

a gun.

FRANK & BILL

A gun.

BILL

Which man is

FRANK

the first man and

BILL

which man has

FRANK & BILL

the gun?

> *FRANK and BILL step back to their chairs and put down their briefcases. They turn their backs on one another and mime pulling guns from their jackets and shooting one another in slow motion. They die elaborately, also in slow motion.*
>
> *The REFEREE blows her whistle. The men leap up. The REFEREE steps down for her judgment. She lifts both their arms in a tie. FRANK and BILL step forward and address the audience.*

I've known this guy for years.

BILL

Years.

FRANK

And this is sad

FRANK & BILL

but it's true . . .

BILL

And when I say years

FRANK

I mean years.

FRANK & BILL

I mean

FRANK

I saw the look of another woman in his father's eyes.

BILL

I smelled the bourbon on his mother's breath.

FRANK

I kept it a secret his aunt was his sister.

BILL

I knew his brother was gay before he did.

FRANK & BILL

I mean years.

FRANK

I mean

BILL

we spent summers together.

FRANK & BILL

Real summers

BILL

when you're a kid.

FRANK

Remember real summers

FRANK & BILL

when you were a kid?

FRANK

It stayed bright till nine o'clock and when it did get dark it got so dark you never wanted to go home.

BILL

Smoking roll-your-owns in the woods with a *Playboy* magazine and warm beer from somebody's father's basement.

FRANK & BILL

No school and Kool-Aid and baseball and hide-and-seek late at night and hot dogs and full moons and overnights outside and swimming.

FRANK

And when they said not to swim alone

BILL

this

FRANK

here

FRANK & BILL

this is the guy I swam with!

BILL

I know this guy better then he knows himself.

FRANK

And that's what makes it sad

BILL

but sad as it is it's true

FRANK & BILL

and the truth of it is:

FRANK

And this is much

BILL

much

FRANK & BILL

much more

FRANK

than something as simple as

BILL

his bad nerves

FRANK

his trouble sleeping

BILL

his shaky marriage

FRANK

his failing business

BILL

his dizzy spells

FRANK

his bad checkups

BILL

his spotty lungs

FRANK

his heart

FRANK & BILL

pa-pa-palpitations.

FRANK

This is

BILL

much

FRANK

much

FRANK & BILL

much sadder than that.

.

FRANK

He's not happy.

FRANK & BILL

He's not happy at all.

BILL

He feels cornered.

FRANK

He feels stuck.

BILL

He feels tied.

FRANK

He feels bound.

FRANK & BILL

He feels trapped.

BILL

And he's a relatively

FRANK

still a relatively young man.

BILL

And I'm just saying that

FRANK

for a relatively young man

FRANK & BILL

that's really sad.

> *FRANK and BILL resume their seats.*

REFEREE

Round Four: Friendly Advice Part One.

> *The REFEREE blows her whistle to begin the round. FRANK and BILL bring their chairs centre and sit.*

BILL

Okay here's the story, these are the facts, this is where I stand, this is the point from which I view the situation.

FRANK

Go on.

BILL

Your situation.

FRANK

Yes.

BILL

I'm not going to pull any punches; I'm not going to cut any corners. I'm not going to give you the short shrift; I'm not going to shovel the shit.

FRANK

The only way to be.

BILL

The only way to be.

FRANK & BILL

Straight up!

BILL

Can I get personal?

FRANK

Personal?

BILL

We're friends.

FRANK

And?

BILL

Well Frank. I've got two good eyes I can't help but see; I've got two good ears I can't help but hear what's being said, and what's being said, around, is . . . Frank, I'm not saying I've got the goods on what makes a marriage work, God knows me and Sally, the honeymoon was over long ago but, Frank . . . it works! And maybe that's just communication and maybe that's just luck but, Frank . . . All I'm trying to say here, buddy, is if you ever need an outside eye, if you ever need a friendly ear, then hey, I'm here.

FRANK rises and stands behind BILL.

FRANK

Are you thinner?

BILL

What?

FRANK

Are you thinner?

BILL

No.

FRANK

You're not thinner?

BILL

No I'm just the same.

FRANK

Really?

BILL

Same as always.

FRANK

It must just be your hair.

> *The* REFEREE *blows her whistle. She steps down for judgment.*
> *She gives the victory to* FRANK. FRANK *and* BILL *move their chairs*
> *from centre.* BILL *sits.* FRANK *steps forward.*

Last Saturday night I'm on the street after before-dinner cocktails
on my way uptown. I flag a cab; I tell him where I'm going; he
says, "Okay." All right. Driving lights, cars, thinking, so on, and

he says something about the night and I say something about the moon and he says something about the weather and I say, "Yeah." The radio on and I say something about the music and he says something about the singer and we both say, "Yeah!" All right. Driving, lights, cars, thinking, so on. Now; on the radio a commercial. "Butter Butter Eat Butter" or something. "Milk Milk Drink Milk" or whatever and he says something about cows and I say something about horses and he says, "Do you like horses?" and I think about it . . . and I think about it and I realize . . . Dammit yes! Yes I do! I have never thought about it before but I am the kind of guy who likes horses. The kind of guy who likes John Wayne and Wild Turkey and carpentry and fishing on lazy August afternoons and horses. Then he says something about the moon and I say something about the night. But you see . . . I like horses. Thank you.

FRANK resumes his seat.

BILL

You're a real cowboy.

The REFEREE blows her whistle twice quickly, calling a foul on BILL.

REFEREE

Round Five: Friendly Advice Part Two.

The REFEREE *blows her whistle to begin the round.* FRANK *and*
BILL *bring their chairs centre and sit.*

FRANK

Seen Phil lately?

BILL

Oh yeah sure.

FRANK

Phil's good guy, eh?

BILL

The best.

FRANK

The best, yes. The kind of guy a guy admires. A guy who's got
it all together. A guy who picks his friends carefully because he
understands a friend is a mirror, a reflection of the thing before it.

BILL

So.

FRANK

I mean . . . look, I'm not going to pull any punches and I don't want you to take this the wrong way but Phil mentioned it and Phil knows we're tight and I'm sure he wouldn't have mentioned it to me if he didn't think I would mention it to you. I mean he likes you. I'm almost sure he does. He thinks you're a fine guy, a good guy, he does, but he mentioned that maybe lately you . . . and I don't . . . I'm only saying this out of concern, as I'm sure Phil was as well . . . but he mentioned that, maybe lately, you've been a little on the—well . . . a bit—how did he put it? A bit too "palpably desperate" I think was his phrase. And, Bill, you can't hold yourself responsible for the fact that business is bad; it's not your fault and tomorrow's another day no matter how bad things seem right now. And Phil is worried, he wouldn't have mentioned it otherwise, and hey, I'm worried too. And I think you should be complimented . . . You should take it as a compliment to your character that a good guy like Phil is concerned about you.

BILL

That's funny.

FRANK

Funny?

BILL

Yeah. He didn't mention it last night.

FRANK

Last night?

BILL

We saw a movie.

The REFEREE moves to end the round. FRANK stops her.

FRANK

Which movie?

BILL

High Noon.

FRANK

What time?

BILL

Seven forty.

FRANK

We're going to the game on Thursday.

BILL

We're going to Montreal for the weekend.

FRANK

We're driving to Arizona for Christmas.

BILL

I'm taking his son camping.

FRANK

He asked me to lend him fifty bucks.

BILL

He wants me to help him build his house.

FRANK

He asked me to be his executor.

BILL

His wife made a pass at me.

FRANK

That dog?

The REFEREE blows her whistle. She steps down for judgment and gives the victory to BILL. FRANK takes his seat. BILL steps forward.

BILL

Not only do I like horses, I love horses; I have ridden horses; I have ridden horses bareback; I have owned a horse; I have seen my horse break it's leg and I have shot my horse. And not only have I shot my horse, I have made love in a stable.

BILL resumes his seat.

FRANK

With who, the horse?

The REFEREE calls a foul on FRANK.

REFEREE

Round Six: Members Only.

The REFEREE blows her whistle to begin the round.

Slowly the men approach one another at centre.

They face one another.

They make the sound of a telephone ringing. They search through their pockets for their cellphones. They answer their phones.

FRANK & BILL

Yeah? Oh hello, sir! Yes, sir.

FRANK

Thank you, sir.

BILL

I'm sorry, sir.

FRANK

Thank you, sir.

BILL

I'm sorry, sir.

FRANK

Thank you, sir.

BILL

I'm sorry, sir.

FRANK

Ha ha ha!

BILL

I-I-I—

FRANK

Thank you—

BILL

I'm sorry—

FRANK

Bobby.

BILL

Sir?—

> *FRANK and BILL hang up. They face one another.*

> *They make the sound of a telephone. They answer their phones once again.*

FRANK & BILL

Yeah?

Hi. I'm in the middle of something right now. Can I—can I—can I call you back?

I don't know.

I told you that. Yes I did. Yes I did this morning. Well it's not my fault if you don't listen. That's right. When I get there.

> *They hang up.*

> *They face one another.*

BILL

Sally says "Hi."

FRANK

Donna says "Hi."

FRANK & BILL

Hi.

> *FRANK and BILL turn to face the REFEREE, their backs to the audience. They take out their penises for inspection. After some deliberation she steps down for judgment as FRANK and BILL tuck in their gear then step down to join her for judgment.*

She calls a tie. Relieved, FRANK *and* BILL *step forward to address the audience.*

FRANK & BILL
"No One Is Perfect."

BILL
By William (Bill) Wade

FRANK
and A. Francis Delorenzo. "No One Is Perfect."

BILL
No one. Were our fathers perfect? Certainly not.

FRANK
Were our mothers perfect?

FRANK & BILL
Perhaps.

BILL
But I am not my mother.

FRANK & BILL

No.

FRANK

Nor is my wife my mother.

BILL

No.

FRANK

Nor will she ever be, as hard as she might try, as much as I might wish she were.

BILL

Frank?

FRANK

I digress. Am I perfect?

BILL

Am I perfect?

FRANK & BILL

No.

FRANK

Yet, let us consider a moment

BILL

a moment

FRANK

that I am not myself

BILL

myself

FRANK

but rather

FRANK & BILL

someone else.

FRANK

Then as this person

BILL

I could

FRANK

watch me

BILL

take note

FRANK

take note

FRANK & BILL

of all the things I do

BILL

the small selfishness

FRANK

the minor idiosyncrasies

FRANK & BILL

the tiny spaces

BILL

between me

FRANK & BILL

and perfection.

FRANK

Perhaps then it would

FRANK & BILL

be easier

BILL

to see

FRANK

to look at me

BILL

and see

FRANK & BILL

be easier

FRANK

to change.

FRANK & BILL

But of course if I was someone else I would have my own problems to deal with.

FRANK

So what is perfect?

BILL

What?

FRANK

Besides tomorrow.

FRANK & BILL

Ah tomorrow!

BILL

Because tomorrow is an endless possibility

FRANK & BILL

and an endless possibility is the second best thing to wake up next to.

FRANK

But what? Let us consider a moment

BILL

a note.

FRANK & BILL

A note.

BILL	**FRANK**
Laaaaaaaaaaaaaaa	At first faltering and self-conscious then
aaaaaaaaaaaaaaa	building up then pushed forward then gaining
aaaaaaaaaaaaaaaa	commitment
aaa . . .	then losing breath and trailing off near the end.

BILL

But in it there was something

FRANK & BILL

perfect.

FRANK

, A happy accident?

BILL

A fluke?

FRANK

Mere chance?

FRANK & BILL

Perhaps. But back to me.

FRANK

And me

BILL

for all my weakness

FRANK

as a note

FRANK & BILL

let's say

BILL

a note stretched out from birth

FRANK & BILL

to death

FRANK

I will allow

BILL

that here and there

FRANK

from time to time

BILL

there is a sound

FRANK

a thought

BILL

a word

FRANK & BILL

that touches on perfection.

BILL

But overall

FRANK

and wholly, no

FRANK & BILL

I know

FRANK

I am not perfect.

FRANK & BILL

I know

BILL

I am not perfect.

FRANK & BILL

But as not perfect as I am he's a whole hell of a lot more not perfect than me.

FRANK and BILL resume their seats.

REFEREE

Halftime.

She blows her whistle.

FRANK and BILL take off their jackets.

The REFEREE comes down centre.

This is the beach. Here is the bay. There is the point.

FRANK and BILL sit on the stage as if on the beach and watch the girl.

This is the beach. Here is the bay. There is the point.
This is the beach. Here is the bay. There is the point.
This is the beach. Here is the bay. There is the point.
Race you to the point?
Sun.
Boys.
Sand.
Water.
Summer.

FRANK
On the beach at the bay.

BILL
Every day that summer.

FRANK

On the beach at the bay.

BILL

All day every day.

FRANK

On the beach at the bay.

BILL

Every day that summer.

FRANK

On the beach at the bay.

BILL

All summer long.

REFEREE

It is the last day of summer before school begins. Two boys and the girl. She lies in the sun in her blue bathing suit on her green beach towel with her yellow radio. And I could tell you little things about her. I could tell you that her name was Lisa. I could tell you that she had a big brother. I could tell you that she loved horses and lilacs and going to the movies. But that doesn't matter now; all that matters is she is here on the beach with the two boys. The boys watch the girl. She stares out past the point to where the sea makes a line on the sky. The boys are silent and shy. She can hear them blush. She reminds one boy of his sister; she reminds the other of a picture of a woman he once saw in a magazine. The boys simply watch the girl.

> FRANK *and* BILL *sing a verse of a summer song.*

The sun hangs about there, just over the point. She is a little drowsy. She gets up and wanders to the edge of the water. She looks out. She feels a breeze. She turns her head a little over her shoulder and speaks to the boys:

"Race you to the point?"

> *Through the following* FRANK *and* BILL *join the* REFEREE *at the edge of the stage.*

This is the beach.
Here is the bay.
There is the point.
This is the beach.
Here is the bay.

There is the point.

There is—

FRANK & BILL

On the beach at the bay.

REFEREE

There is—

FRANK & BILL

On the beach at the bay.

REFEREE

There is—

FRANK & BILL

On the beach at the bay.

REFEREE

There is—

FRANK & BILL

On the beach at the bay.

REFEREE

There is the point.

FRANK

And we sat

BILL

on the sand

FRANK

at the edge

BILL

of the point

FRANK

and we waited

BILL

and waited.

REFEREE

Race you to the point?

(to FRANK) Do you remember?

FRANK

One.

> *FRANK assumes a racing position.*

REFEREE

(to BILL) Do you remember?

BILL

Two.

> *BILL assumes a racing position.*

REFEREE

I remember too.

I remember. Three!

> *The REFEREE blows her whistle to end halftime. The men return*
> *to their chairs and put on their jackets. Perhaps they change*
> *sides, as in a sporting match.*

Recap: Two men enter a room, a taller man and a shorter man, and each man carries a briefcase. The first man seems very much like the second man and the second man seems very much like the first man, but they are not.

FRANK & BILL

No.

REFEREE

They are not for two reasons. One: one man is the first man, and two: one man in his briefcase has a gun.

BILL

A gun.

FRANK

A gun.

REFEREE

Which man is the first man and which man has the gun?

> *The REFEREE returns to her chair.*

Round Seven: Dad.

> *The REFEREE blows her whistle to begin the round. FRANK and BILL approach one another at centre. FRANK does the what's-on-your-tie gag to BILL, ending in a nose flick. BILL shoves FRANK. FRANK shoves BILL. BILL shoves FRANK, knocking him down. The REFEREE calls a foul on BILL. FRANK and BILL circle one another.*

FRANK

How's your dad?

BILL

Why?

FRANK

I always liked your dad.

BILL

Really?

FRANK

Yeah.

BILL

Well. I always liked your dad.

FRANK

Really?

BILL

Yeah.

FRANK & BILL

Gee.

FRANK

Your dad was a real easygoing guy.

BILL

Your dad was a real card.

FRANK

Your dad was a real dreamer.

BILL

Your dad was a real character.

FRANK

Your dad was a real nice guy.

BILL

He was a real maniac.

FRANK

He was a real boozer.

BILL

Ha. He was a real wild man.

FRANK

A real cuckold.

BILL

A real wiener.

FRANK

A real dick.

BILL

A real prick.

FRANK

A lemming.

BILL

A fascist.

FRANK

An ass.

BILL

A pig!

How's your mom?

> *The REFEREE blows her whistle. She steps down for judgment.*
> *She calls a tie.*

> *FRANK and BILL simultaneously speak the following duologue.*
> *The capitalized phrases time out to be spoken in unison.*

FRANK

Please be warned that if you think I'm going to stand here and start dishing dirt and airing laundry about HIS FATHER, I won't. But let's just say the desperation he displays comes from HIS FATHER. Not that I'm sure he wasn't a well-intentioned, ill-educated man, and education isn't everything, but FOR EXAMPLE: Rather than face the criminal charges HIS FATHER implied he could not multiply eight times nine when HIS FATHER's company was missing some seventy-two thousand dollars at the year-end audit. HIS FATHER claimed he had marked down twenty-four. Twenty-four? Give me a break. AND THAT'S JUST ONE EXAMPLE. Dishonest? Well he did admit to an ignorance in arithmetic and WELL I'M SURE YOU KNOW WHAT THEY SAY ABOUT FATHERS AND SONS, and far be it, far be it indeed for me to say that HE IS THE PERFECT EXAMPLE. THANK YOU.

BILL

Now this is more than name-calling here, although of course that is the temptation, but HIS FATHER drove his mother crazy; I mean she did have a drinking problem but HIS FATHER didn't help at all. She spent the last fifteen years in and out of detox as a result of his antics. FOR EXAMPLE: At the Girl Guide Boy Scout banquet in grade eight HIS FATHER was supposed to make a presentation, but when the time came HIS FATHER was nowhere to be found. Twenty minutes later five guys from the sixth pack found HIS FATHER in the boiler room with Suzie Walsh a sixteen-year-old Girl Guide. AND THAT'S JUST ONE EXAMPLE. Is he like that? Well they say a guy and his father are, WELL I'M SURE YOU KNOW WHAT THEY SAY ABOUT FATHERS AND SONS, and I'm not saying they're right all the time, but in this case HE IS THE PERFECT EXAMPLE. THANK YOU.

FRANK and BILL move to resume their seats.

REFEREE

One more time.

FRANK and BILL return to centre.

As they are about to begin:

And twice as fast.

> *FRANK and BILL take a moment then repeat the duologue at twice the speed. When they are finished they move back to their chairs.*

Thank you.

FRANK & BILL
You're welcome.

REFEREE
Round Eight: The Big Brain or the Big Heart.

> *The REFEREE begins the round. FRANK and BILL come to centre. They face one another.*

FRANK
You've got auction preferreds yielding seventy percent of prime and 50/51 up either side; what do you want to do? Convert with three-year hard-call protection, two-year payback, the hedge is a layup? I don't think so. I say capitalize the loss by rolling it into goodwill and amortizing over forty years. Of course profits will be decreased by the switch from FIFO to LIFO. And then remember Bethlehem! Where application of FASB 87 meant balance-sheet quality went way down because of the unfunded pension liability.

I mean if we were in another situation I could offer at one half and give up an eighth to the market maker for three eighths net fill, but unfortunately we're not. Are you with me?

BILL

Did you know I broke my foot last year?

FRANK

You broke your foot?

BILL

Yes I did. Do you want to know how?

FRANK

How did you break your foot?

BILL

I fell out of a tree trying to save a kitty-cat.

REFEREE

Awwww.

> *The REFEREE blows her whistle. She steps down for judgment and gives the victory to BILL. FRANK resumes his seat. BILL steps*

forward. As he speaks he stands in one position but points and
steps and turns in place as indicated.

BILL

Let's go to my place, everybody. Okay. Ready?

This is the back door.

We always use the back door.

Here is the rec room. There is the bar. There is the laundry room.

Hallway, stairs. Going up stairs, going down stairs.

Out that window that's the yard.

Here's a hallway. There's the kitchen.

Microwave, butcher's block, breakfast nook.

Hallway. Turn.

Dinning room.

Oak table, eight chairs, hallway, French doors, living room.

It's sunken!

Big window.

Big skylight.

Grand

piano

(white).

Through the hallway into the foyer.

Front—

We never use the front door.

Window, window, powder room.

MASSIVE STAIRCASE!

One. Two. Three. Four. Five bedrooms. (Can in two.)

Long hallway. Smaller staircase.

Going up stairs. Going up stairs. Going up stairs.

Door. Locked. Key. Open the door. And this

is my secret room.

FRANK

I heard you rent.

> *The REFEREE calls a foul on FRANK. BILL speaks to FRANK without looking at him.*

BILL

Where'd you hear that?

FRANK

Around.

BILL

Yeah?

FRANK

Yeah.

BILL

Around where?

FRANK

Just around.

BILL

Phil?

FRANK

Might've been Phil.

BILL

Phil's full of shit.

> *BILL returns to centre. This time as he speaks he stands and delivers the speech without moving.*

As I was saying. This is my place. Back door rec room bar laundry out that window that's the yard kitchen hallway turn dining room turn living room turn hallway MASSIVE STAIRCASE one two three four five bedrooms hallway staircase. Going up stairs going up stairs going up stairs door locked key open the door and this is my secret room. And this is my secret room. And this is my secret room. And it's empty except for a great big window right here, and when I look out of it I see the tops of trees, and hills, black roads with white lines, and a whole lake, and two kinds of earth: dark wet earth and clay, and big green fields and sky that's only ever blue. And all of it. Everything. Theskythefieldsthetreesthelakethehillstheroadtheclay. Everything I see, and farther where you can't see, all of it, everything, is mine. It's all mine.

BILL resumes his seat.

REFEREE

Round Nine: Power Lunch.

The REFEREE blows her whistle to begin the round.

FRANK and BILL bring their chairs centre. They sit facing one another.

FRANK

Been here before?

BILL

Oh yeah.

FRANK

How's the steak?

BILL

Very good.

FRANK

How's the swordfish?

BILL

Very good.

FRANK

How's the shark?

BILL

Greasy.

FRANK & BILL

Excuse me a second.

> *FRANK and BILL reach into their pockets and take out their phones. They dial and both make a ringing sound. As BILL speaks FRANK continues to ring.*

BILL

Hi, doll!

Listen sorry I was short with you before.

Did you go ahead and have dinner anyway?

Ahhh . . . Well how 'bout I pick up a pizza on my way home?

And a movie?

Something funny?

Something romantic! That sounds nice!

Okay, turnip.

I do too.

Bye bye.

> *FRANK and BILL hang up.*

How's Donna?

> *Pause.*

How's—

FRANK

I heard you. She's very good.

BILL

Really?

FRANK

Yes. How's the spaghettini?

BILL

Oily. I saw Donna at the Fuller's party.

FRANK

Oh yes.

BILL

You weren't there.

FRANK

No I wasn't.

BILL

Phil was there.

FRANK

Was he?

BILL

He was having a good time.

FRANK

Good.

BILL

So was Donna.

FRANK

Donna likes a good—

BILL

Party?

FRANK

Yes.

BILL

I've heard that.

FRANK

How's the squid?

BILL

Sneaky.

FRANK

Sneaky?

BILL

Sneaks up on you. Nice tie.

FRANK

Yes you mentioned—

BILL

Somebody has good taste.

FRANK

How's Sally?

BILL

Very good.

FRANK

Really?

BILL

She was at the Fuller's. Strange you weren't there.

FRANK

Well I wasn't.

BILL

"Working late"?

FRANK

I don't believe you've ever had the steak or the swordfish or the shark or the spaghettini or the squid here.

BILL

No I haven't.

(to the audience) But it was a good party.

> *The* REFEREE *blows her whistle. She steps down for judgment and gives the victory to* FRANK.

Bullshit call!

> *The* REFEREE *calls a foul on* BILL. BILL *resumes his seat.* FRANK *steps forward.*

FRANK

Let's not use the word "class." Class being such a nebulous word. Let's instead use "mountain." Mountain. And many men are born without a mountain. It is not a birthright. This is not to say that a mountain is particularly better than a valley—just as we may find from time to time that knowledge is not particularly better than ignorance. And even being second has its benefits. For example . . . less income tax? But some men live on mountains and some men live in valleys and if only those men standing small and insignificant in the valley would stop their futile fight to stake a claim at the crest of a hill they can never hope to own. If only they would not be so blind and for a moment consider the privilege of living in the benevolent shadow of a mountain. But to be brave enough to see that truth and face it, that takes balls, and like mountains many men are born without them.

BILL

Fuck you, Alphonse.

The REFEREE calls a foul on BILL.

FRANK

You slimy little—

The REFEREE calls a foul on FRANK.

REFEREE

Round Ten: Business Ties.

> *The REFEREE begins the round. FRANK and BILL step centre. FRANK faces the audience. BILL faces FRANK and stands at an uncomfortably close distance.*

FRANK

Now I don't want to harp on business, Bill, but I happen to be pretty tight with Bobby and Bobby runs everything and I now how things are with you and there's a chance that there might be a place opening up in accounting from what I've heard—

BILL

Frank, I really like that tie.

FRANK

And from what I've heard about business, Bill—

BILL

Silk? Of course. How could I imagine Donna would buy a tie like that?

FRANK

I'm offering you a break here, Bill, I'm—

BILL

That's not Donna's taste.

Very flashy.

Yet tasteful.

Where would a person buy a tie like that?

What kind of store?

FRANK

Bill . . .

BILL

What kind of person would go into that kind of store and buy a tie like that?

FRANK

Don't, Bill.

BILL

A very young tie!

FRANK

Shut up about the goddamn tie!

> *FRANK resumes his seat. The REFEREE blows her whistle. She steps down for judgment and gives the victory to BILL. BILL steps forward.*

BILL

Two stories. The first story is a very familiar story because everybody knows it. And it's a story about a little temp, eighteen years old, who is, by the way, knocked up and who happens to have not bad taste in ties, don't you think? And the second story is a secret so just keep it to yourselves. We're at the Fuller's party. Me and Sally. Huge spread, packed bar, beautiful house, the works. Tons of people, people everywhere. There's Donna! Where's Frank? Frank's not here. Donna's there though. She looks great! Who's that she's talking to? It's Phil. I wander over. They're talking about politics. I wander off. Have a drink, have a chat, check out the pool, come back in, poke around some more at the buffet, shoot the shit . . . Phil and Donna still talking! I cruise over. Now they're talking about poetry. I cruise off. Time comes to go, Sally's pulling on my arm; I'm talking to Mr. Fuller. Look around for Donna to say goodbye . . . No Donna. Look around for Phil . . . No Phil. I gotta take a pee before we leave, walk in the can. There's Donna. In the shower. With Phil. And when she sees me she smiles and says: "Shh! Come on in and close the door, Bill." Now the first story you can repeat but the second story, *(whispering)* that's a secret.

     BILL resumes his seat.

REFEREE

Round Eleven: My Boy.

> *The REFEREE begins the round. FRANK and BILL step to centre.*
> *They do a simple choreography of hand gestures.*

FRANK & BILL

Let me tell you something about my boy.

He's a good boy, my boy.

A good boy, a smart boy.

> *FRANK, flummoxed, stops.*

BILL

He's the best boy, no question.

> *BILL stops and looks at FRANK.*

FRANK

(to the REFEREE) Sorry.

FRANK & BILL

Let me tell you something about my boy.

He's a good boy, my boy.

A good boy, a smart boy.
He's the best boy, my boy.

>	*FRANK stops and turns away*

BILL
No question he's the—

(to FRANK) Are you with us?
What's your problem? Hey. Hey. What's your problem?

>	*BILL looks at the audience, shrugging.*

FRANK
Password.

>	*BILL does not respond.*

Password.

>	*BILL does not respond. FRANK takes off his jacket.*

Winner rules.

BILL

(to the REFEREE) That's not in the game.

> *FRANK steps to centre.*

FRANK

Password.

> *BILL takes off his jacket and joins him at centre.*

BILL

Winner rules.

> *FRANK and BILL do a childhood handshake.*

FRANK & BILL

Cut! Spit! Mix! Brothers brothers never part, no broken vows
of covered hearts, in all our weakness, all our woes, we stick
together, highs and lows.

FRANK

Pledge?

BILL

Made.

FRANK

Promise?

BILL

Kept.

FRANK

To what end?

BILL

Never end. Transit! Transport!

> *FRANK and BILL join hands, raising their arms over their heads, forming an arch. The REFEREE walks through this and down centre.*

One.

FRANK

Two.

REFEREE

Three.

> *FRANK, BILL and the REFEREE begin to swim.*

FRANK, BILL & REFEREE

Cut through the water to the point. Cut through the water to the point.

Cut through the water to the point. Cut through the water to the point.

> *The three continue to swim, and the men continue speaking the above as the REFEREE speaks.*

REFEREE

I'll beat you. I'm a good swimmer. You guys think you're so hot. My brother taught me to swim and he's on a team. What's your names anyway? My name's Lisa. My mom calls me Leelee but I hate that. What's your names anyway? You guys got a cottage here? You brothers? We've got a cottage up by the store on the hill; you know where I mean? It used to be a farm but we don't have any animals. I wish we had a horse; I love horses. I go to the movies on Sunday. I go every Sunday even if it's one I saw already. Hey slow down, it's far. Slow down.

FRANK & BILL

And I feel her fall back. And I feel her fall back. And I feel her fall back. And I feel her fall back.

> *FRANK and BILL continue the above while:*

REFEREE

What's your names? Hey. Wait. Let's not race. Wait. We're too far. Slow down. Hey. Wait. Hey . . .

> *Through the following* REFEREE *text* FRANK *and* BILL *continue swimming while* BILL *speaks "And I feel her, I feel her fall back" and* FRANK *resumes "Cut through the water to the point."*

His decision.

His compassion.

His desire.

His jealousy.

His guilt.

His self-image.

His self-knowledge.

His self-loathing.

His fear of death.

His weakness.

His pride.

His power.

> *The men continue swimming but are silent as:*

And first there is panic.

And so much sound.

Rushing.

Swirling.

Pulsing.

And then no sound. And then peace. And then you will float or you will sink. And if you float you will be as if flying and if you sink, when you hit bottom, you will bounce like a man on the moon.

The REFEREE *returns to her chair.*

FRANK & BILL

Cut through the water to the point.

Cut through the water to the point.

Cut through the water to the point.

Cut through the water to the point.

FRANK *slowly raises his arms in victory.* BILL *continues to swim.*

FRANK *walks toward* BILL.

BILL

Cut through the water to the point. Cut through the water to the point.

Cut through the water to the point. Cut through the water to the point.

BILL rises as he continues to speak. FRANK places his hand on BILL's shoulder.

Cut through the water to the point. Cut through the water to the point.
Cut through the water to the point. Cut through the water to the point.

FRANK and BILL are now standing face to face. With his other hand FRANK punches BILL in the stomach. BILL goes down.

The REFEREE blows her whistle. She steps down for judgment and gives the victory to FRANK. BILL struggles to his feet and approaches FRANK. FRANK address the audience.

FRANK
I'd like to make a few things clear. These are my ears; these are my eyes; this is the back of my hand.

FRANK strikes BILL with the back of his hand. BILL goes down.

And the winner has, and will always, rule. That is the way of the world. Like battle, like business, like love. A few may fall along the way but compared to the prize, what are a few. And the prize is what you want and what you want is what you hear in every mouth, every buzz, every bell, every crack, every whisper: "Me, my. Mine." Don't be afraid. The thing we must learn is how to balance compassion and desire. For example: Bill? You like this tie?

FRANK takes his tie off and puts it around BILL's neck.

Have it.

FRANK yanks on the tie.

Say thank you. Say thank you!

BILL
(choking) Thank you.

FRANK drops BILL to the floor.

FRANK
No thanks necessary, Bill; I've got a dozen just like it at home. You see. Don't be fooled.

FRANK lifts BILL and supports him.

Beware compassion. Compassion will lose the race. Compassion is illogical. If you let it compassion will kill desire. Especially the desire to be first. And being first, my friends, is the point.

FRANK throws BILL across the room.

Compassion is the brother of guilt.

FRANK lifts BILL by his tie.

And guilt is the mother of stomach cancer.

FRANK knees BILL in the stomach.

The first man is the man

FRANK knees BILL in the chest. BILL goes down.

who is guiltless beyond all circumstance

FRANK kicks BILL.

and sure of his right

FRANK kicks BILL.

to be first.

FRANK kicks BILL.

The first man is the man

FRANK kicks BILL.

who can recognize the second man.

BILL lies motionless. FRANK steps forward.

And we sat on the sand at the edge of the point and we waited and we waited and you got scared and you ran home and all night long I waited and in the morning when her body washed up on the shore I tried to comfort her but she did not respond, then to evoke some reaction I slapped her so hard my hand still hurts. And then learning my lesson I declared myself first to the point.

FRANK resumes his seat.

REFEREE
Round Twelve: Rumours of Glory.

FRANK steps to centre. BILL tries to struggle to his feet. The REFEREE calls a foul on BILL. BILL continues to struggle. The REFEREE calls a foul on BILL. BILL continues to struggle. The REFEREE blows her whistle to end the round. She steps down for judgment and gives the victory to FRANK. FRANK steps forward. BILL manages to get to his feet. He approaches his briefcase.

FRANK

I have always been, will always be, the first.

FRANK resumes his seat. BILL opens his briefcase, takes out a gun and aims it at FRANK.

BILL

And I learned my lesson, Frank. I won't be second again.

FRANK, surprised, opens his briefcase. FRANK takes out a gun and aims it at BILL.

FRANK

The game's not over yet, Bill

The REFEREE steps forward and addresses the audience. She holds a yellow radio.

REFEREE

The two men will stand here just like this for a long time to come with one thought. One thought racing through each man's mind:

FRANK & BILL

Somebody lied.

Somebody lied.

Somebody lied.

The men continue to speak "somebody lied" through the following.

REFEREE

Two boys on a beach. The last day of summer before school begins. Nearby is a girl. She lies in the sun in her blue bathing suit on her green beach towel listening to her yellow radio. She reminds one boy of his sister; she reminds the other of a picture of a woman he once saw in a magazine. The sun hangs about there. Just over the point. She turns her head a little over her shoulder and speaks to the boys: "Race you to the point?"

The men stop speaking.

And they do. One two three. The boys are afraid. The boys are still afraid. Round Thirteen:

The men cock their guns.

Only One Gun Is Loaded.

> *She whistles to begin the round. The men look at her in disbelief, still keeping aim. She places the radio on the stage, turns it on. She drops her whistle on the stage and exits the way the men came in. The radio plays a happy beach song. The men look at one another, still keeping aim. Lights fade.*

> *The End*

This Is A Play

In memory of Doug Cowan

This Is A Play was first produced by da da kamera and the Fringe of Toronto at the Bathurst Street Theatre in June and July of 1992. It featured the following cast and creative team:

Female Actor: Caroline Gillis
Older Female Actor: Judith Orban
Male Actor: Daniel MacIvor
Voice of the Composer: Ed Fielding

Directed by Ken McDougall

Characters

Female Actor
Older Female Actor
Male Actor
Composer (voice only)

The Style

The actors are at all times acting the "play" (which I have given the title *No Stranger Among Us*), so that even when the actor is actually speaking to the audience about what is happening in his or her head there is a sense of another text being played out as well—this is best shown by the actor's going through the blocking of the "play" no matter what they are speaking. The SMALL CAPS dialogue is text from the play. The Composer should exist as a taped voice and not be performed live. The Composer's text may be revised and cut in order to accommodate the pace of individual productions.

Notes are included where productions may make adjustments to text that reflect production values or changes in popular culture.

Bare stage. Black.

COMPOSER

(voice-over) This is an original score. This score has been created especially for this piece and not only is it an original score in the sense that it has been created for this piece specifically but also in the sense that it is undeniably original.

> *Light up.* FEMALE ACTOR *is on stage. She gazes dreamily off.* OLDER FEMALE ACTOR *enters.*

OLDER FEMALE ACTOR

THERE'S A COLD WIND BLOWING IN OFF EAST BAY.

FEMALE ACTOR

I'LL GO FETCH YOUR SHAWL, AUNTIE.

OLDER FEMALE ACTOR

NO NO, GIRL, SIT SIT. LETTUCE IS COMING UP REAL NICE OUT BACK.

FEMALE ACTOR

SIX FIFTEEN SHOULD BE PASSING THROUGH SOON.

OLDER FEMALE ACTOR

OH SISSY, YOU'RE ALWAYS WAITING FOR THAT TRAIN. YOU SPEND YOUR WHOLE LIFE WAITING. SITTING LIKE SOME LITTLE BIRD. SITTING LIKE SOME GLASS BIRD ON A SHELF WAITING FOR THAT TRAIN. WAITING.

FEMALE ACTOR

OH AUNTIE.

> *The sound cue is late.*

OLDER FEMALE ACTOR

Waiting. For that train.

> *The sound of a train whistle (this can be made by the MALE ACTOR off stage or it can be recorded).*

FEMALE ACTOR

THERE IT IS. OH AUNTIE, IT'S STOPPING!

OLDER FEMALE ACTOR

NOW WHO'D BE FOOLISH ENOUGH TO GET OFF HERE?

MALE ACTOR enters and crosses down carrying a suitcase.

FEMALE ACTOR
(still gazing out) A STRANGER.

OLDER FEMALE ACTOR
A STRANGER?

> *MALE ACTOR and FEMALE ACTOR turn to face one another. They slowly walk backwards and away from one another and off stage.*

(to audience) Confused by the moody lighting and the empty stage?* Nervous because you were expecting a comedy? "Oh no," you think now, "it's experimental!" Relax. You know me. I'm the older, but still attractive, female actor; wise and gruff and charming, rough around the edges but soft on the inside. I am a mother image for the playwright, but a more perfect mother, not like his own who never really understood his delicate artistic sensibilities. And now I deliver my first monologue. It is a story about three heads of lettuce that were separated and how they ended up, three lonely heads of lettuce: one in a kitchen, one in a market and one in the back of a produce truck. A story

---

*   If your production has a set she should say "hokey set."

that asks the question: Will they ever reunite? You worry again wondering if this might be children's theatre. It should be. You look at your watch and shift in your seat and I'm out of here.

OLDER FEMALE ACTOR exits.

MALE ACTOR
(off stage) I enter with conviction!

MALE ACTOR enters and crosses the stage, tripping a bit midway.

I take up a position stage right. I am sick with embarrassment. Not only did I trip on my first big cross but now I am not in my light. I find my light. I look out at the audience, but just over your heads so as not to destroy your suspended disbelief, and I wonder what to do with my hands. I think about winning a Tony[*] and begin a speech about *lettuce* and every time I say the word *lettuce* I say it with great emphasis because the writer told me to. My story is about one lonely *lettuce* in a kitchen, then talk about my recently dead brother, then hint at this mysterious mission type thing I'm on. I don't understand this speech but I manage to fake it. Then I move my arms in a strange way because the

---

[*] Rather than say "Tony" you may insert here a local theatre award for acting.

director has a dance background. Then once again I mention *lettuce*. Then silence. I exit!

MALE ACTOR exits. FEMALE ACTOR enters.

FEMALE ACTOR

Tentatively I enter, gracefully moving my arms in a strange way because the director has a dance background. Immediately and professionally I scan the audience quickly out of the corner of my eye and wonder if my mother is here. I think about art and begin my monologue. It is a story about lettuce—one lonely lettuce in a market—a monologue that would be a total embarrassment if it weren't for the brilliant emotional motivations given me by the director, my mentor. I continue, once again mentioning lettuce and then leap to noting my relationship to the older female actor, who is currently smoking in the *non-smoking* green room. Now I take up a strong position centre and wait for the entrance of my leading man, the empty-headed monster.

MALE ACTOR

(off stage) I enter with conviction!

MALE ACTOR enters.

I think about Jake Gyllenhaal* and look away and wait for her to look at me.

FEMALE ACTOR

I'm sure he must be thinking about Jake Gyllenhaal.

MALE ACTOR

I wait for her to look at me.

FEMALE ACTOR

I wait for as long as possible and then I look at him.

MALE ACTOR

I look at her.

FEMALE ACTOR

I think: I wish they'd cast someone better looking.

MALE ACTOR

I think: She thinks I can't act.

---

* You may insert here any famous young male actor of the moment—or perhaps a famous young actor who resembles the actor playing the MALE ACTOR—either way, if the name changes it should change throughout the text.

FEMALE ACTOR

I think: He can't act.

MALE ACTOR & FEMALE ACTOR

Focus!

FEMALE ACTOR

I take my time. I let the audience drink me in. I feel pretty. I do a quick little spin and with tentative interest look at him with a question in my eyes.

MALE ACTOR

I look at her. She's got that weird look on her face again. I snap myself out of it by thinking about stardom and speak my lines with some anger and great conviction.

FEMALE ACTOR

I respond with annoyance at his response to my questioning look.

MALE ACTOR

I respond with confusion to her strange reaction to my response to her weird look after my great conviction.

FEMALE ACTOR

I react shrilly to his confused response to my annoyance with his aggression toward my quick little spin and my tentative questioning look.

MALE ACTOR

I forget what I'm supposed to do next.

FEMALE ACTOR

He probably forgets what he's supposed to do next so I pause.

Pause.

MALE ACTOR

I remember.

MALE ACTOR & FEMALE ACTOR

I cross the stage like a caged animal. I take up a position ever so slightly away from yet ever so slightly toward. Pain, hope and fear dance across my face in a delirious symphony.

MALE ACTOR

I pause.

FEMALE ACTOR

He's not supposed to take this pause. The director told him a hundred times this pause is not needed.

MALE ACTOR

In the pause I act really hard.

FEMALE ACTOR

You're dragging the play down; you're milking the moment; you're killing the momentum; you're pissing me off.

MALE ACTOR

With excellent acting now mustered I upstage her and say my line.

FEMALE ACTOR

I fix my great hair; I upstage him back and I refuse to say my line.

MALE ACTOR

I think: She's blanked.

FEMALE ACTOR

I wait. I make him sweat.

MALE ACTOR

I sweat.

FEMALE ACTOR

I say my line.

MALE ACTOR

I'll never take that pause again.

FEMALE ACTOR

I ask him a rhetorical question.

MALE ACTOR

I answer her rhetorical question.

FEMALE ACTOR

I tell him it was a rhetorical question.

MALE ACTOR

WHAT'S A RHETORICAL QUESTION?

FEMALE ACTOR

WHY, IT'S A QUESTION THAT'S GOT NO ANSWER OF COURSE. DIDN'T YOU LEARN THAT IN SCHOOL?

MALE ACTOR

I LEARNED THAT QUESTIONS HAVE ANSWERS.

FEMALE ACTOR

SOME DON'T.

MALE ACTOR

WHAT KIND OF QUESTIONS DON'T HAVE ANSWERS?

FEMALE ACTOR

THE QUESTIONS FROM OUR HEARTS.

MALE ACTOR

IF ONLY I HAD A HEART.

FEMALE ACTOR

EVERYBODY'S GOT A HEART.

MALE ACTOR

DO THEY? WHAT'S YOUR NAME? I'M JOEY.

FEMALE ACTOR

I'M SISSY.

MALE ACTOR

SISSY. I BET YOU'VE GOT A HEART THOUGH, *(touching her arm)* DON'T YA, SISSY.

FEMALE ACTOR

DON'T TOUCH ME; DON'T YOU EVER TOUCH ME! YOU CAN'T TOUCH ME. I'M MADE OF GLASS AND YOU'RE A STRANGER HERE. AUNTIE! AUNTIE! AUNTIE!

OLDER FEMALE ACTOR enters.

OLDER FEMALE ACTOR

FOR THE LOVE OF GOD AND ALL THE SAINTS IN HEAVEN, WHAT IS IT, GIRL?

FEMALE ACTOR

OH AUNTIE, THERE'S A STRANGER AMONG US!

OLDER FEMALE ACTOR

WHERE? WHO IS HE? WHO ARE YOU? WHAT ARE YOU DOING TO MY NIECE?

OLDER FEMALE ACTOR & FEMALE ACTOR

Blackout!

Blackout.

MALE ACTOR

(in the black) Blackout!

COMPOSER

(voice-over) But then again what is an original composition? What is original? If the art is an extension of the artist, and if each person is an original being, then doesn't it just follow that even the most banal, indulgent and derivative work—

> *Light up. OLDER FEMALE ACTOR stands centre holding a bowl of soup.*

OLDER FEMALE ACTOR

Silence. A long silence. A very long silence as I stand here holding a bowl of soup for no good reason other than for you to imagine what a good-hearted, folksy and simple person I am. And while you think that, I think about the other two now off stage congratulating themselves on their overwrought performances. Suddenly I become deeply sad about not being in a better wig. Finally I speak. A perilous journey over dry and dusty terrain explaining things you already know—that the girl is my niece and the boy is a stranger. I smile. I continue the exposition—talking to whom I'm not quite sure because the director insists I'm talking to God and the writer insists I am talking to myself . . . and lost for a moment in that accidental profundity I struggle for focus . . .

MALE ACTOR
(off stage) I enter with great conviction!

OLDER FEMALE ACTOR
And here comes Jake Gyllenhaal.

MALE ACTOR enters.

MALE ACTOR
I think about Jake Gyllenhaal and wait for her to say her first line. I glance at her and see that she's in one of those trances again. I try not to panic and get into her line of vision.

OLDER FEMALE ACTOR
I gently take him by the arm and lead him to his light.

MALE ACTOR
I think: Why is she dragging me around the stage?

OLDER FEMALE ACTOR
I feed him his first line.

MALE ACTOR

I say my first line.

OLDER FEMALE ACTOR

I smile and finally get to say my first line.

MALE ACTOR

I say my second line.

OLDER FEMALE ACTOR

I say my second line.

MALE ACTOR

I say my third line.

OLDER FEMALE ACTOR

I say my third line.

MALE ACTOR

I say my fourth line.

OLDER FEMALE ACTOR

I say my ninth line.

MALE ACTOR

I look at her funny.

OLDER FEMALE ACTOR & MALE ACTOR

Focus!

MALE ACTOR

I say my sixth line.

OLDER FEMALE ACTOR

I say my fifth line.

MALE ACTOR

I say my third line again.

OLDER FEMALE ACTOR

I say my tenth line.

MALE ACTOR

I . . . tell her my name.

OLDER FEMALE ACTOR

I act like that name means nothing to me.

MALE ACTOR

I speak her name.

OLDER FEMALE ACTOR

I turn away.

MALE ACTOR

I speak her name, not call her name. I'm not sure what the difference between speaking and calling is but it says in the script, "He speaks her name, not calling," and the writer says what I do is perfect.

OLDER FEMALE ACTOR

I fix my eyes upon him with great contempt.

MALE ACTOR

I think she hates me.

OLDER FEMALE ACTOR

I turn away.

MALE ACTOR

Relieved, I tell this cute little story about a dog I used to have. It's not supposed to be here but it was cut from my first monologue and the writer and the director had a big fight about it and so I get to say it now. I think the writer really likes me.

OLDER FEMALE ACTOR
I look at him with curiosity and think about how much saliva he has.

MALE ACTOR
I worry that I might be spitting.

OLDER FEMALE ACTOR
I feel sorry for the people sitting in the front row.

MALE ACTOR
I finish off about the dog and I mention my brother and then I congratulate myself on my good acting. I see a casting director sitting in the third row. I wish they'd kept that part in where I take off my shirt.

OLDER FEMALE ACTOR
I lead him through his blocking and wonder what the writer sees in him.

MALE ACTOR
I think: Why is she dragging me around the stage again.

OLDER FEMALE ACTOR

I wait for his line, which mentions his brother's name.

MALE ACTOR

I wait for her line.

OLDER FEMALE ACTOR

He thinks it's my line.

MALE ACTOR

It's her line. Isn't it?

OLDER FEMALE ACTOR

I say a line that's not in the script.

MALE ACTOR

That line's not in the script.

OLDER FEMALE ACTOR

Even though it makes no emotional sense to my character whatsoever I outright ask him what his brother's name is.

MALE ACTOR

Oh right! I mention my brother's name.

OLDER FEMALE ACTOR

WHY, THAT NAME MEANS NOTHING TO ME.

MALE ACTOR

HE'S DEAD.

> *OLDER FEMALE ACTOR gasps.*

WHAT IS IT?

OLDER FEMALE ACTOR

NOTHING, JUST . . . DEATH ALWAYS MAKES ME GASP.

MALE ACTOR

IS THAT ALL?

OLDER FEMALE ACTOR

OF COURSE.

MALE ACTOR

LOOK AT ME! LOOK AT ME! DON'T I REMIND YOU OF SOMEONE?

OLDER FEMALE ACTOR

NO! YOU STAY AWAY FROM ME. AND YOU STAY AWAY FROM MY NIECE. THAT GIRL IS FRAGILE; YOU HURT HER AND I'LL BREAK YOU. YOU MARK MY WORDS.

MALE ACTOR

I can't believe they couldn't find her a better wig. I come downstage and say something poetic.

OLDER FEMALE ACTOR

I give him the bowl of soup.

MALE ACTOR

I take the bowl of soup.

OLDER FEMALE ACTOR

And I'm out of here.

> *OLDER FEMALE ACTOR exits.*

MALE ACTOR

She wasn't supposed to give me the bowl of soup.

> *FEMALE ACTOR enters.*

FEMALE ACTOR

Tentatively I enter. Everything I do is tentative because I understand my character to be tentative and so everything I say or do is said and done in a tentative way. Tentative yet tense. A tense tentativeness. But can tension be tentative? Can tentativeness be tense? Have I based my whole character on an emotional impossibility? Am I a fraud? Is that why my mother never comes to see my plays? Why is he holding a bowl of soup?

MALE ACTOR

I offer her the bowl of soup.

FEMALE ACTOR

I ignore him and begin my monologue. I tell a story about my childhood and talk in poetic imagery about summer and sea air. I talk about a boy I remember.

COMPOSER's voice comes in under FEMALE ACTOR.

A boy in short pants and freckles. I lose my place. I think: Why does the score have to come in here. I become self-conscious. Maybe if the writer spent more time working on the script rather than chasing down interviews we wouldn't need to hide the words by playing something over them! I feel like I'm yelling!

COMPOSER

(voice-over) Of course in terms of originality we have to ask the question how can anything be original beyond the first thought, the first idea? It is as if the first impulse to art was original art and then every impulse after this is an interpretation, a facsimile if you will, making none but the original original original.

MALE ACTOR

I've got to get a copy of that score.

FEMALE ACTOR

Now suddenly I think about my first acting teacher, how she told me I barked all my lines and how I hated her. I wonder if it's unhealthy to build an entire career on spite. I lose my place. I don't feel happy. I'm supposed to be happy in this moment. I try to think about something happy. I remember last night at the director's apartment—his beautiful eyes, his manly hands, that look in his eyes. I know that he loves me and we will be together forever. Silently I dedicate my performance to him. I continue on now about my childhood, summer and sea air. Then I tentatively mention lettuce. I compliment myself internally for a beautiful performance and I wait for him to say his line.

MALE ACTOR

I think: She must be sleeping with the director.

FEMALE ACTOR

I shoot him a look.

MALE ACTOR

LETTUCE? WHAT WAS THAT ABOUT LETTUCE?

FEMALE ACTOR

NOTHING JUST . . . I'VE GOT SOMETHING AGAINST LETTUCE. I HATE IT.

MALE ACTOR

FUNNY, SO DO I.

FEMALE ACTOR

DO YA?

MALE ACTOR

YEAH, I DO.

FEMALE ACTOR

SORRY I GOT SO UPSET BEFORE. IT'S JUST THAT I'M . . .

MALE ACTOR

FRAGILE?

FEMALE ACTOR

YEAH. AND, I GOT A PAST.

MALE ACTOR

EVERYBODY'S GOT A PAST, SISSY.

FEMALE ACTOR

DO THEY?

MALE ACTOR

YEAH THEY DO.

FEMALE ACTOR

GEE, I FEEL LIKE YOU KNOW ME.

MALE ACTOR

DO YA?

FEMALE ACTOR

YEAH I DO.

They move in slowly to kiss.

Blackout.

They are closer to kissing.

Blackout!

They are almost kissing.

Blackout!

Blackout.

COMPOSER

(voice-over) But is originality even enough? What about concept? What about content? And how do I know that someone in Berlin or Japan hasn't created an original score exactly like this original score, making neither original?

Light up.

OLDER FEMALE ACTOR

(off stage) I take my time entering because I feel like it.

OLDER FEMALE ACTOR enters.

I begin a monologue you can tell was stuck in after previews because no one in the audience could understand what the hell was going on. Relentless exposition peppered with lame humour. And since I'm alone on stage again and no one's really listening anyway I leave out a paragraph of particular purpleness. Later I'll say I forgot it and apologize, and I will be forgiven because they expect that from the older female actor and her fading memory. Now from out of nowhere: *(singing)* "I sing a few lines from an old Scottish ditty / To try and distract from the writing so shitty / And the non-existent connection to / The next shoddy section." Then I stop suddenly. I hear them coming. I react and leave the stage in a manner that indicates that I'll be watching them from somewhere.

OLDER FEMALE ACTOR *begins to exit.*

But I won't.

OLDER FEMALE ACTOR *exits.*

MALE ACTOR *and* FEMALE ACTOR *enter holding hands.*

FEMALE ACTOR
His hand is so clammy. I begin, tentatively at first, my favourite monologue. It's a lovely monologue full of images and metaphors drawn from modern psychology and nature creating a philosophy of functional spirituality. And then I look at him with a look that

lets him know that he is everything to me—my life, my love, my future. I try not to gag or sound ironic.

MALE ACTOR

I get an impulse.

FEMALE ACTOR

Oh no, he's got an impulse!

MALE ACTOR begins to take off his shirt.

MALE ACTOR

I slowly begin to take off my shirt.

FEMALE ACTOR

I try to pretend he is not taking off his shirt.

MALE ACTOR

First I pull it from my pants and then undo each button from the bottom, filling my eyes with hazy possibilities. I bet that casting director will hire me now.

FEMALE ACTOR

I pray for a blackout.

MALE ACTOR

I suck in my gut and think about Jake Gyllenhaal.

FEMALE ACTOR

I'm sure he's thinking about Jake Gyllenhaal.

MALE ACTOR

I realize I probably shouldn't be thinking about a guy right now.

FEMALE ACTOR

I wonder if he's gay?

MALE ACTOR

I wonder if I'm gay?

MALE ACTOR & FEMALE ACTOR

Focus!

MALE ACTOR

I stare at her with passion.

FEMALE ACTOR

I cannot meet his eyes.

MALE ACTOR

I stare!

FEMALE ACTOR

I can't!

MALE ACTOR

I stare!

FEMALE ACTOR

I can't!

MALE ACTOR

I stare!

FEMALE ACTOR

I can't.

MALE ACTOR

We wait.

FEMALE ACTOR

We wait.

MALE ACTOR & FEMALE ACTOR

We wait.

OLDER FEMALE ACTOR enters. FEMALE ACTOR gasps.

MALE ACTOR

We gasp!

OLDER FEMALE ACTOR

I stand centre as if I have something important to say.

MALE ACTOR

I look at her with defiance mixed with shame.

FEMALE ACTOR

I look at her and wonder why they couldn't find her a better wig.

OLDER FEMALE ACTOR

I look at him. I look at her. I wonder: Did I leave my cigarette burning?

ALL

Blackout!

Blackout.

COMPOSER

(voice-over) Or perhaps there is a wave of thought that is shared by all creators, tuning in and out of one another's ideas. Does this account for instances of innocent plagiarism such as occurred on that classic episode of *The Partridge Family* when Danny—

Light up.

OLDER FEMALE ACTOR

Fascinatingly, the scene begins in the middle of an argument.

MALE ACTOR

I say something I don't understand.

FEMALE ACTOR

I say something he doesn't understand.

OLDER FEMALE ACTOR

I say something that makes sense of what they said and I manage to make the line funny even though it isn't.

MALE ACTOR

And now—

FEMALE ACTOR

—a bit—

OLDER FEMALE ACTOR

—of Mamet—

FEMALE ACTOR

—esque—

MALE ACTOR

—dia—

OLDER FEMALE ACTOR

—logue.

MALE ACTOR

Clipped—

FEMALE ACTOR

—and frac—

OLDER FEMALE ACTOR

—tured—

MALE ACTOR

—and—

FEMALE ACTOR

—highly—

OLDER FEMALE ACTOR

—enter—

MALE ACTOR

—tain—

FEMALE ACTOR

—ing.

OLDER FEMALE ACTOR

Or so—

MALE ACTOR

—thinks—

FEMALE ACTOR

—the writer.

OLDER FEMALE ACTOR

And now a sentence brimming with brutal imagery stolen from early Judith Thompson.*

ALL

I wish someone would do *White Biting Dog*** again; that's a perfect part for me!

FEMALE ACTOR

I implore her!

MALE ACTOR

I beseech her!

OLDER FEMALE ACTOR

I ignore him.

FEMALE ACTOR

I challenge her.

---

* If your audience is not fortunate enough to be familiar with the brilliant Canadian playwright Judith Thompson, who wrote many plays including *White Biting Dog*, *The Crackwalker* and *Lion in the Streets*, then you may substitute "Tennessee Williams" here.

** As above, you may substitute with *The Glass Menagerie*.

OLDER FEMALE ACTOR

I evade her.

FEMALE ACTOR

I corner her.

MALE ACTOR

I beseech her!

OLDER FEMALE ACTOR

I shun him.

FEMALE ACTOR

I accuse her!

MALE ACTOR

I beseech her!

>   *OLDER FEMALE ACTOR and FEMALE ACTOR look at the MALE ACTOR*
>   *disdainfully.*

I implore her?

FEMALE ACTOR

(to MALE ACTOR) I implored her already.

MALE ACTOR

(to FEMALE ACTOR) I challenge her?

OLDER FEMALE ACTOR

(to MALE ACTOR) She did that.

MALE ACTOR

(to FEMALE ACTOR) I beg her?

FEMALE ACTOR

(to MALE ACTOR) Fine.

MALE ACTOR

I beg her!

FEMALE ACTOR

I take all the focus now; you drink me in. I, tentatively at first, begin to try not to cry, holding it back, holding it back, holding it back—I don't want to cry, I don't want to cry—holding back, holding back, *(weeping theatrically)* but the tears rush forward and words roll out that explain the argument we were just having and then brings attention around to his brother.

MALE ACTOR

With startling conviction, even to myself, I threaten to say what I know.

FEMALE ACTOR

With feigned courage I dare him.

OLDER FEMALE ACTOR

A stunned silence from me.

MALE ACTOR

I speak as if entranced because that's what the script says I should do. I talk about my dead brother and his deathbed message about a woman named Auntie. Now I'm supposed to cry about my brother. Of course I myself never had a brother and so I use the Uta Hagen Substitution Method that I heard those two talking about last week. I'm trying to substitute my dead cousin but I never liked my cousin and I'd rather substitute Mr. Whiskers, my cat who died, but it seems kind of dumb to substitute a cat for a person *(growing emotional)* . . . but I guess the point of it is not if it's a cat or an armadillo or whatever, just that it's somebody you wish never went away . . . *(weeping)* . . . I miss you Mr. Whiskers.

OLDER FEMALE ACTOR & FEMALE ACTOR

I think: He must be sleeping with the writer.

OLDER FEMALE ACTOR

All right! I begin an endless and pointless story about my girlhood full of that salty, wheezing humour you've grown so used to. Then more drivel about my gritty adolescence and then a hint about a secret, and finally a chance to do a little acting . . . *(just on the edge of tears, but not crying)* . . . I won't cry; I won't cry; I won't cry.

MALE ACTOR & FEMALE ACTOR

God she's good.

OLDER FEMALE ACTOR

And then more sap until from out of nowhere, and using every trick I have been ashamed to see another actor use, I skilfully bring it around to . . . lettuce.

FEMALE ACTOR

I look at him.

MALE ACTOR

I look at her.

OLDER FEMALE ACTOR

I look at them.

MALE ACTOR

WHAT'S ALL THIS TALK ABOUT LETTUCE ANYWAY?

FEMALE ACTOR

AUNTIE HAS A FONDNESS FOR LETTUCE.

OLDER FEMALE ACTOR

I ALWAYS HAVE, GIRL; YOU KNOW THAT.

MALE ACTOR

WELL I HAVE THIS.

> *MALE ACTOR rolls up his sleeve, exposing a tattoo. FEMALE ACTOR gasps.*

OLDER FEMALE ACTOR

(knowingly, without looking) A LETTUCE TATTOO.

MALE ACTOR

HOW'D YOU KNOW . . . ?

FEMALE ACTOR

THAT LETTUCE TATTOO . . . IT'S JUST LIKE . . .

> *FEMALE ACTOR exposes her own tattoo.*

MALE ACTOR

MY GOD! YOU'VE GOT ONE TOO! AND SO DID MY BROTHER. WHAT DOES IT MEAN? WHAT DOES IT MEAN?

FEMALE ACTOR

WHAT DOES IT MEAN, AUNTIE? WHAT DOES IT MEAN?

> *MALE ACTOR and FEMALE ACTOR move toward and away from one another in dance-like movements. This continues throughout OLDER FEMALE ACTOR's speech until noted.*

MALE ACTOR & FEMALE ACTOR

We move together. We move apart. We move together. We move apart. We move together. We move apart.

OLDER FEMALE ACTOR

And now I step forward to wrap things up—but God knows why since no effort was made to crate a plausible plot. Nevertheless, I explain that as a girl I had triplets—those two and the dead brother. I marked all three with a lettuce tattoo and gave the boys to a foster home and only the recently dead one knew about it, and so on and so on and more exposition.

> *MALE ACTOR and FEMALE ACTOR stop and watch OLDER FEMALE ACTOR.*

But then comes the last line of the monologue, and although it is somewhat corny I like to say it because it makes me feel like I'm on stage, and reminds me why I do this job. And also the title of the play is the line and that seems to make me the star. This line:

SO NO MORE SHADOWS, NO MORE LIES, NO STRANGER AMONG US.

FEMALE ACTOR
OH JOEY!

MALE ACTOR
OH SISSY!

> *They embrace her.*

MALE ACTOR & FEMALE ACTOR
OH MAMMA!

Blackout!

Blackout.

COMPOSER

(voice-over) Which brings us to: Who owns an idea? Yes, who indeed. Ultimately, and I suppose this is a symptom of the business society, it is the person who pays for the idea who owns the idea.

> *Light up. The three actors are on stage, in a line, facing out, their hands behind their backs.*

OLDER FEMALE ACTOR

Here we stand.

MALE ACTOR

Each of us alone.

FEMALE ACTOR

Yet a group.

MALE ACTOR ·

I find my light.

FEMALE ACTOR

I fix my hair.

MALE ACTOR

We do our best to muster meaning in this pause.

FEMALE ACTOR

I make a statement that seems somewhat out of character, thus indicating a change.

OLDER FEMALE ACTOR

So do I.

MALE ACTOR

So do I.

OLDER FEMALE ACTOR

And then.

FEMALE ACTOR

From behind our backs.

MALE ACTOR

Each of us.

FEMALE ACTOR

Produce.

OLDER FEMALE ACTOR

A lettuce.

FEMALE ACTOR

A lettuce.

MALE ACTOR

A lettuce.

OLDER FEMALE ACTOR

And in this strange, almost surreal gesture there is some kind of clarity.

FEMALE ACTOR

And inexplicably for a moment.

OLDER FEMALE ACTOR

Each of us.

FEMALE ACTOR

Each of us.

MALE ACTOR

Even me.

OLDER FEMALE ACTOR

Seems to understand.

ALL

Something.

OLDER FEMALE ACTOR

And as the lights fade.

FEMALE ACTOR

I think about Uta Hagen.

MALE ACTOR

I think about Jake Gyllenhaal.

FEMALE ACTOR

I think about Jack Daniels.

ALL

Because we are actors.

OLDER FEMALE ACTOR

And this.

FEMALE ACTOR

This.

MALE ACTOR

This.

OLDER FEMALE ACTOR

This is a play.

> *They make a strange dance-like movement in unison and the light fades as:* ·

COMPOSER

(voice-over) And that is the end of this original score. *(slightly off-mic, as if to somewhat in the recording booth)* Okay that should be enough. If you need more just start it over from the beginning. Now can we talk about money? Seriously though?

The End

Daniel MacIvor is one of Canada's most accomplished playwrights and performers. Winner of the prestigious Elinore and Lou Siminovitch Prize, the GLAAD Award, the Governor General's Literary Award, and many others, Daniel's plays have been met with acclaim throughout North America.

First edition: December 1993. Second edition: February 2016.

Printed and bound in Canada by Imprimerie Gauvin, Gatineau

Cover photo of Robert Dodds and Daniel MacIvor © Michael Lo
Author photo © Guntar Kravis

PLAYWRIGHTS CANADA PRESS

202-269 Richmond St. W.

Toronto, ON

M5V 1X1

416.703.0013

info@playwrightscanada.com

www.playwrightscanada.com

A bundled eBook edition is available
with the purchase of this print book.

CLEARLY PRINT YOUR NAME ABOVE IN UPPER CASE

Instructions to claim your eBook edition:
1. Download the BitLit app for Android or iOS
2. Write your name in **UPPER CASE** above
3. Use the BitLit app to submit a photo
4. Download your eBook to any device

RECYCLED
Paper made from
recycled material

FSC
www.fsc.org   FSC® C100212